RICK JACOBSON

The Master's Apprentice

Illustrated by

LAURA FERNANDEZ & RICK JACOBSON

TUNDRA BOOKS

Published in Canada by Tundra Books,
75 Sherbourne Street, Toronto, Ontario M5A 2P9

Published in the United States by Tundra Books of Northern New York,
P.O. Box 1030, Plattsburgh, New York 12901

Library of Congress Control Number: 2007927390

LIBRARY AND ARCHIVES CANADA CATALOGUING IN PUBLICATION
Jacobson, Rick
    The master's apprentice / Rick Jacobson ; illustrated by Rick Jacobson
and Laura Fernandez.
ISBN 978-0-88776-783-8
    1. Michelangelo Buonarroti, 1475-1564–Juvenile fiction. I. Fernandez, Laura
II. Title.

PS8619.A26M37 2008   jC813'.6   C2007-902738-5

OA ONTARIO ARTS COUNCIL
    CONSEIL DES ARTS DE L'ONTARIO

We acknowledge the financial support of the Government of Canada through the Book Publishing
Industry Development Program (BPIDP) and that of the Government of Ontario through
the Ontario Media Development Corporation's Ontario Book Initiative. We further acknowledge
the support of the Canada Council for the Arts and the Ontario Arts Council for our publishing
program.

The illustrations for this book were rendered in watercolor.

Design: Kelly Hill

Printed and bound in Singapore

1   2   3   4   5   6   13   12   11   10   09   08

"The greater danger for most of us
lies not in setting our aim too high and falling short;
but in setting our aim too low, and achieving our mark."

Michelangelo Buonarroti

Thanks to:

Francesco Cesario

Peter Parente

Alex Fregoso-Gonzalez

Jeff Bessner

Greg Manion

"Are you afraid, Marco?" The words trembled in the fading darkness.

Marco paused before answering his brother.

"No." Even as he said it, his stomach knotted. Then half to himself he added, "It's a great honor."

Dawn crept farther into the room. Marco remembered the shadowed canals of Venice. He missed them already. Venice was a city of mystery and secrets, while Florence was a city of light.

The family had come only yesterday to Florence, upon learning that Marco would be junior apprentice to the young Michelangelo Buonarroti. For this opportunity, Marco's father had labored hard as a chemist, mixing artists' colors – colors prized for their brightness and clarity. He had done well, but now his son would do even better.

The family set out. With each step, Marco thought, *Not yet, not yet* . . . Then came the last corner, and there was the house. His mother's tears and his brother's awkward handshake spoke louder than words. It would be a long time before Marco would see them again.

His father embraced him with hurried words. "Be careful, my son. This Buonarroti has an evil temper, but he has much to teach you. Listen. Learn. Remember what I have taught you. Above all," he said through a thin smile, "keep our secrets secret."

Suddenly alone, Marco knocked on the door.

The door swung open and there stood a boy, not much older than himself.

"*Buon giorno*. I'm Marco. I –"

"I'm Ridolfo. You're late! You were expected at sunrise." The boy's voice was full of venom. He turned and walked away.

Marco followed close behind. "Where is the master?" he inquired between steps.

"Everyone is at the Hospital of the Dyers, of course. *Il Divino* is preparing his cartoon for the fresco."

"Cartoon?" Marco repeated.

"Don't you know anything?" Ridolfo sneered. "A cartoon is a large drawing the master prepares before painting a fresco."

They passed the stable courtyard. The odor told Marco the horses had been neglected for some time. The boys climbed a set of stairs and entered a large room.

"You will sleep there." Ridolfo pointed to a pile of seed bags in the corner. "Tomorrow you will go with the others to the hospital. Today you will clean the stables."

It was evening before each stall was clean and laid with fresh straw. Marco's hands were sore and he smelled. He washed up and went inside, hungry for supper. Ridolfo was already eating.

"Those stables had better be spotless," he said through a mouth full of food.

The banging of the door and footsteps on the stairs announced the master's return. There was no doubt that the man who entered was Michelangelo. He was short and stocky, bearded and dirty, but his eyes were as sharp as his temper was said to be.

Ridolfo leapt to his feet, and approached Michelangelo. They spoke in hushed tones as Marco stood nervously under the cold stare of his new master.

"If you think you are here to be my new stable boy, think again. You will be on time and do as you are told, or I will send you back to your father in disgrace."

Before Marco could speak, Michelangelo was gone. Ridolfo followed, looking pleased with himself. Marco was more frightened than ever before.

Marco didn't sleep well on the cold, damp floor. Before dawn, Ridolfo appeared.

"Il Divino wants you to go to the chemist and choose his ultramarine."

Marco was wary. Ultramarine was the most expensive color. Why would the master trust him with such an errand after yesterday's poor start? "Does the master intend to begin painting already?" he asked.

"It is not up to you to question anything! Just do it!"

Marco had to obey. Reluctantly, he set out. Ridolfo's directions were unclear and Florence was new to Marco. Before long, he was lost. After asking several people, he finally reached the chemist's shop.

"I am here to choose ultramarine for Michelangelo Buonarroti," he said.

The man looked surprised at first, then burst out laughing. "Michelangelo can have ultramarine when he has the money to buy it." He was still laughing as Marco left.

Marco arrived at the Hospital of the Dyers late, and worse, empty-handed. Michelangelo was competing with his bitter rival, Leonardo da Vinci, the most famous genius in all of Italy. The stress was showing on everyone. Marco entered quietly, trying to be invisible.

Those eyes missed nothing. "Where have you been?" Michelangelo bellowed. "I thought I made myself clear last night!"

Ridolfo stood by the door, smiling, as Marco tried to explain. "Ridolfo sent me to pick up the ultramarine –"

"Is it likely I would trust you with that? Where is Ridolfo?"

Marco looked toward the door, but the boy was gone.

To Marco's great relief, he was not sent home. Ridolfo disappeared for two days and Marco began to wonder if it was the older boy who had been sent away.

When Ridolfo did return, he seemed ashamed and avoided Marco's eyes.

It is no easier for him to be apprenticed to this master than it is for me, thought Marco. He wanted to say something kind. Instead he said, "You're back."

Ridolfo hesitated for a moment. "I'm sorry," he said.

Marco smiled. "At this rate, we will both be sent home."

The two apprentices spent the afternoon preparing the wall for the fresco.

At work the next day, everyone watched as Michelangelo stared at the letter in his hand. The courier was from Rome. The letter was from the pope himself. Everyone knew what it meant. Michelangelo would be called to Rome. It was a call he could not easily ignore.

"What will happen with the fresco?" Marco asked.

"It will not matter now," Ridolfo whispered. "The master will send everyone away, except for one or two." The cold tone was back in Ridolfo's voice. Marco mistook it for fear.

He, too, was terrified. "I mustn't be sent home!"

Ridolfo brightened. "You know the science of colors," he said. "Why not mix something special for him? Try scarlet. He loves scarlet. You will have to hurry."

Marco had helped his father prepare alizarin crimson many
times. It was the most glorious red. The recipe was simple and
Marco knew the ingredients by heart. On a hill overlooking Florence, he
found the weedy plant he needed in abundance. He dug an armful of the root
and headed back to the studio. It took the rest of the day to boil it down to
the red liquid he needed. Early the next morning he had a pot of fine
crimson, but Michelangelo was nowhere to be found.

    "He's carving. The studio is just around the corner," Ridolfo said.
"Why not take it to him?"

Marco knocked and waited. He was about to leave, when the door flew open and a hideous face glowered at him. Michelangelo had worked through the night. When the light failed, he had worn a hat ringed with candles. He stood now, full of rage, covered in marble dust and wax.

"What do you want?" he demanded.

"I mixed crimson for you." Marco held the pot out. Michelangelo didn't even look at it.

"You interrupt me for crimson? I never use crimson! Any fool knows that." The door slammed in his face.

Ridolfo was waiting when Marco returned. The haughty look and the smirk were back. "Did Michelangelo like his crimson?" he asked.

Marco was in despair. His father had done everything to get him this chance, and now he would most certainly be sent home. He thought of the advice his father had given him in their last, hurried embrace. Suddenly, he knew exactly what he should do. It was dangerous, but he had watched his father carefully. He could do this.

"I guess only one of us will be going to Rome after all."

Marco ignored Ridolfo. Without a word he left in search of poison.

As Marco went about gathering and preparing the ingredients, he could hear his father's voice. *Be careful not to breathe the fumes. Make sure it doesn't get too hot.*

Marco smiled as the color emerged. It was perfect. His father would have been proud.

Michelangelo was standing with a group of men who had come to see the cartoon. Though the fate of the fresco was in doubt, they were very complimentary. The master was in rare, good spirits. Marco waited patiently.

"What is it?" Michelangelo asked. At once, all eyes were on Marco.

"I have something to show you, master," Marco held out the still-warm pot of color. Michelangelo looked into it, then quickly up at Marco. "That's emerald green! Where did you get this?"

"I mixed it myself, master. My father taught me."

The others crowded around, knowing how difficult it was to make this hue properly.

Michelangelo studied the color. "Why does it glimmer?"

"That is a family secret. I cannot tell you, master."

"You will have no secrets from me!" Anger glinted in the artist's eyes. He was no longer happy.

The room was silent. Ridolfo smiled in the corner. Everyone waited for Marco's response. Here was his chance to go to Rome, but to seize it would mean betraying his father. Marco took a deep breath.

"I'm sorry, master. I can give you the paint, but I cannot tell you how I made it. I promised my father I would not."

To everyone's surprise, there was no angry outburst. Michelangelo turned away. Marco's heart was heavy. How could he tell his father he had failed?

In the upstairs room, Marco gathered his things. It wasn't long before Ridolfo entered.

"Il Divino has sent for you." He gloated as Marco passed. "Say hello to Venice for me."

Michelangelo was making his own travel arrangements when Marco entered the studio. "Are you ready to tell me your secret now?"

"I cannot, master. I am free to give you the color, but not the recipe. I would guard your secrets as carefully, if you asked me to."

"This is your last chance. I will take only one apprentice to Rome. Would you disgrace your father?" Michelangelo's back was to him.

"My father will know I did not fail him." Marco was surprised at the strength of his voice.

"The commission from the pope is an important one. Your color skills will be useful to me . . . but your loyalty will be priceless." Michelangelo turned, and for the first time, he smiled at Marco. "Get your things. You are going to love Rome."

ive hundred years after this story, Michelangelo Buonarroti is celebrated as one of the greatest painters and sculptors of all time. His huge fresco on the ceiling of the Sistine Chapel and his *Last Judgment* over the chapel's altar are perhaps his most renowned works. Together they took a total of ten years to complete.

But in 1503, Michelangelo was a young man who had just sculpted his masterwork, *David*. It was no surprise when he was commissioned to paint a wall in the Palazzo Vecchio in Florence. The surprise came when Leonardo da Vinci was commissioned to paint the facing wall. This was a competition!

The great genius of Leonardo was already established. He had just completed his *Mona Lisa* and he took the competition as an insult.

Florence buzzed with speculation. Who would begin first? What would each man paint? Whose work would be judged the best?

Leonardo started painting first, but his fresco, *The Battle of Anghiari*, was never finished. He had experimented with a paint recipe that turned out to be disastrous. In some places the fresco turned black. In others it melted. Leonardo left Florence.

Michelangelo finished his cartoon, but never started painting because he was summoned by Pope Julius II to begin the Sistine Chapel.

Perhaps fate played a part in keeping works by the two artists from facing each other for centuries to come. Leonardo and Michelangelo were simply beyond compare. That they lived and worked in the same city at the same time was as remarkable as the works they left behind.